DOLLARS & SENSE

TEACHING FINANCE & WISDOM

Dollars & Sense

Teaching Finance & Wisdom

This book shares knowledge, perspective, and lessons to inspire smarter financial decisions. It is not intended to replace personalized advice. Always consider your own circumstances when making financial choices.

Any names, characters, or scenarios used are for illustrative purposes only and may be fictionalized to enhance understanding.

First Edition

ISBN: 979-8-9944522-0-2

Publisher: Buystorm

Cover design by Buystorm

Printed in the United States of America

About the Author

Greg is a father of four, a man shaped by experience, and a storyteller committed to truth. At 52, he's lived through the consequences of questionable decisions and the lessons they carry. His greatest priority has always been family, ensuring his children, born to three different mothers, grow up with strong bonds, shared memories, and a deep understanding of what it means to show up for one another.

Through years of reflection and growth, Greg recognized that love alone isn't enough, our youth also need tools. Dollars & Sense was born from that realization: a guide not just for his children, but for every young person navigating the challenges of finance, legacy, and self-worth. With a focus on wealth-building, responsibility, and the power of community, Greg offers practical wisdom wrapped in lived experience.

His mission is clear: to teach, uplift, and empower one story, one lesson, one generation at a time.

DEDICATION

To my children Kimora, Skylar, Liam, and Andre who inspire every lesson in this book.

To their mothers, Nicole, Trina, and Falon thank you for shaping their hearts and helping them see their father's vision for family, finance, and wisdom.

And to every young reader: may this book remind you that your mind is your greatest asset, your time is your most valuable currency, and your discipline is the key to wealth.

BOOKS
FREEDOM
MIND
OPEN
DAY
STORM
TAKE THE

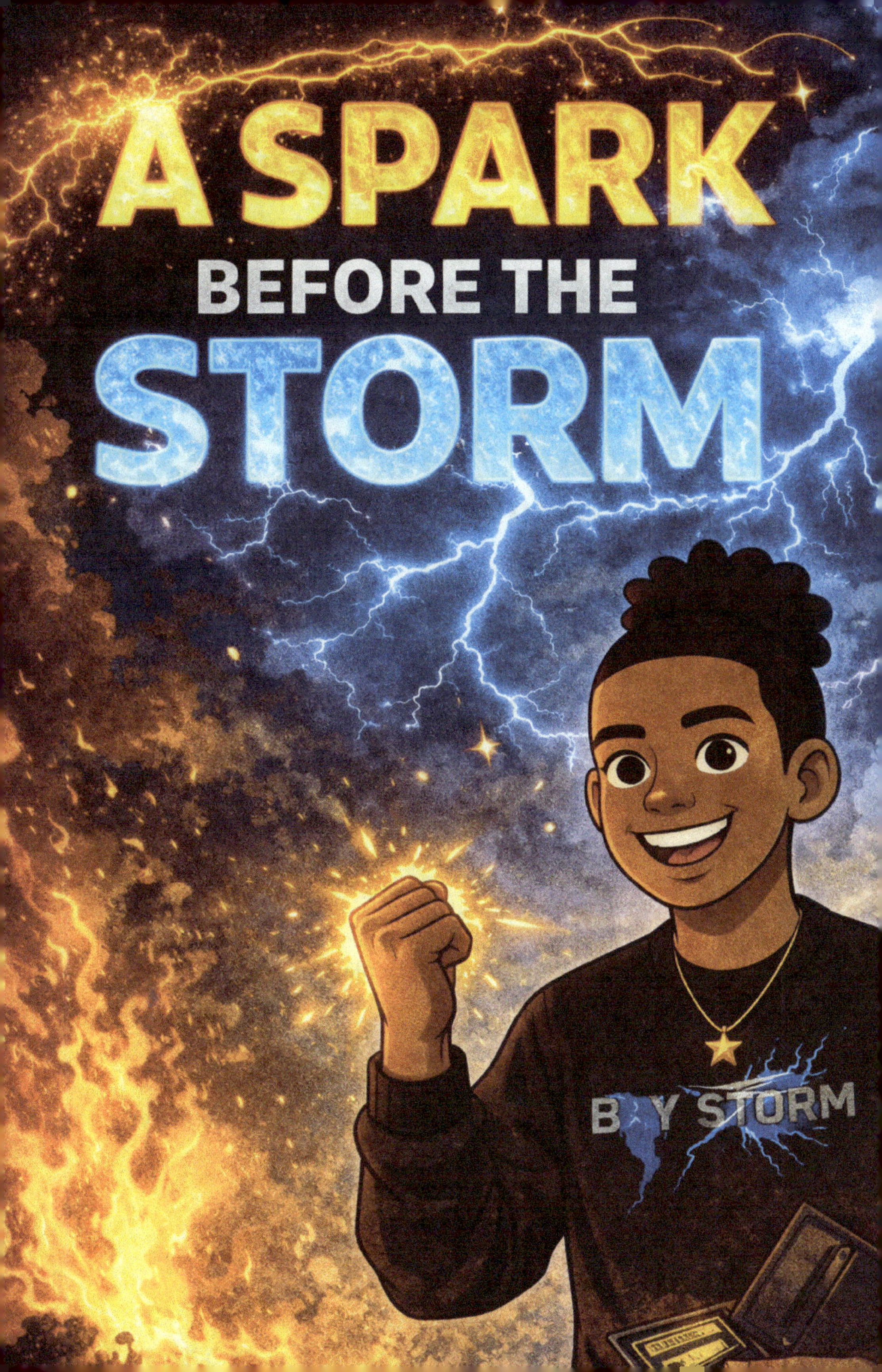
A SPARK
BEFORE THE
STORM

A Spark Before the Storm

The sun dipped low over Hollis, Queens, casting golden light across boarded-up storefronts and cracked sidewalks. Sky stood on the steps of the community center that had seen better days. Her eyes scanned the faded mural of the best DJ in the U.S. of A.

“Yes… this is the exact place we need,” she whispered.

Liam appeared beside her, arms crossed, eyes sharp. “We need more than just an old building. We need a plan.”

Sky grinned. “I got one, a pop-up thrift market. We collect donations, sell what we can, and use the profit to repair this place.”

Liam raised an eyebrow. "And what if no one shows up? What if we spend more than we make?"

From behind them, Andre laughed. "Then we'll learn something. You can't win if you don't start."

Kimora chimed in, "And if we do win, we prove that young people can rebuild their own community."

Sky said, "We need to go big, live show, music, lights, something that can make people feel the heartbeat of this place."

Liam: "It costs money to make all of those things happen."

Sky: "That we don't have yet."

Sky (smiling): "But we will. This is how we start strong."

Liam: "Or how we crash before we take off."

Andre: "I saw a system on the stage back there. I can rig the basic sound system for free nothing flashy, but it works."

Kimora: "I can have Dad talk to Dave to get his rapper friends for exposure."

Sky: “I just want it to be unforgettable.”

The basement was colder than usual. Andre had just finished rewiring the old fuse box when his flashlight flicked across a loose brick in the wall. Curious, he pried it free, and behind it was a dusty, leather-bound book.

“Sky!” he called. “You need to see this!”

They gathered around as Andre carefully opened the cover. Inside were pages filled with handwritten notes, dates, and numbers.

Sky: “Whoa… it’s a blueprint for building wealth.” The energy was electric.

Liam: “Wait is this real? Financial advice, and this thing’s got handwritten notes about history?”

Andre: “Yo, this is wild! It’s got wealth-building investment breakdowns, and even legacy planning. Whoever wrote this was serious about passing down wealth.”

Kimora: “This isn’t just a book. It’s a playbook. We could use this to teach workshops, build programs.”

Sky: “This book was left here for a reason. Maybe they wanted someone like us to find it.”

Liam: “Or maybe they were trying to protect it. Look at these notes, “Generational wealth begins with knowledge.” That’s deep.”

Andre: “Check this out, there’s a section on family and having each other’s back. Exactly what we were talking about leading into this project.”

Kimora: “There’s a timeline of economics, financial stability, as well as history. I really enjoyed the historical aspect of the book.”

Sky: “We need to digitize this, share it. This could be the foundation of our financial literacy program.”

Liam: “Imagine if we host a Legacy Lab, where teens learn from this book and build their own wealth plan.”

Andre: “Let’s do it. The book’s not just history, it’s a future waiting to be written.”

They weren't just learning about money.

They were learning about purpose, partnership, and possibilities.

This was the spark that would ignite everything.

TABLE OF CONTENTS

DOLLARS & SENSE & TEACHING FINANCE AND WISDOM

Chapter 1: Repeat Daily The Power of Habits

Greatness doesn't appear overnight; it's built one decision at a time.

What you do daily shapes who you become.

When Sky set out to organize her pop-up thrift market, she didn't start with money. She started with discipline, waking early, making lists, following through.

Liam learned to track donations. Andre handled repairs. Kimora focused on presentation. Each small task, repeated every day, built consistency, and consistency builds confidence.

Lesson for Readers

Repetition creates results.

If you study, save, or practice a skill daily, success becomes a habit, not a dream.

Activity

Write down one thing you want to improve this month, saving, studying, helping, or learning and do it every single day for 21 days. At the end, reflect on how your habits changed your mindset.

Repeat Daily

I'm in school to get the tools I need to build something on my own one day.

Like a business that can give other people jobs.

That way, I can help others provide for their families while also providing for mine.

Repeat Daily
I'm in school to get the tools I need to build something on my own one day.
Like a business that can give other people jobs.
That way, I can help others provide for their families while also providing for mine.
SAVING

Chapter 2: Understanding Assets vs. Liabilities

That Saturday morning, Sky looked at the old speaker sitting on the center's stage.

“If we fix it, we could rent it out for parties,” she said.

Liam laughed. “Who's gonna rent that thing? It's older than us!”

But Andre wasn't laughing. “It's not about what it looks like, it's about what it can do.”

Kimora pulled out her notebook and wrote two columns: Assets and Liabilities.

They decided to test the concept. Andre repaired the speaker using wires from an old stereo. It worked. They listed it online and earned $100 from one weekend rental.

Lesson learned:

The broken speaker became an asset because it brought in money but if they had bought a new one they couldn't afford, it would have been a liability.

What's the Difference?

Assets put money into your pocket.

Liabilities take money out of your pocket.

Assets and Liabilities:

Assets

Assets are things that put money in your pocket or grow in value.

Examples: savings account, stocks, business, rental property, education.

Liabilities

Liabilities are things that take money out of your pocket or lose value over time.

Examples: credit card debt, car loans, expensive clothes, or unused subscriptions.

Assets feed you. Liabilities drain you.

Examples

Items	Asset or Liability?	Why?
Gaming Console	Liability	Takes money and doesn't earn anything
Camera used for YouTube	Asset	Can make income through videos
Expensive sneakers	Liability	Lose value once worn
Stock Investment	Asset	Grow in value, earns dividends

Activity: Feed It or Drain It?

Make two boxes labeled ASSET and LIABILITY. Write down items (like phone, car, savings account, business, debt) and place each where it belongs. Discuss why.

Key Takeaway

Wealthy people focus on buying assets that grow and produce income.

Impoverished people collect liabilities that look good but cost them money.

Teen Affirmation

"I build assets, not debt. My money works for me, not the other way around."

Examples

A bike used to deliver groceries =Asset

A bike you never ride = Liability

A phone used for endless scrolling = Liability

A phone used for business = Asset

Challenge

Look around your room. Write down 3 things you own.

Ask yourself:

Does it earn, or does it drain?

Be honest the answer will reveal how you view money.

Chapter 3: The 50/30/20 Rule & Smart Budgeting

After the thrift market and mini concert earned $5,000, Sky said, "Yes! I knew it could be big. We have our original $1,000 plus $4,000 more. We must thank Dave. Fab really gave us the spark we needed."

Liam shook his head. "Yeah, that was tough. Let me get my $250 back now."

Andre nodded. "Same here. I saw some new sneakers I want to buy."

Kimora snapped her fingers. "Bros, relax! We must reinvest and save. We've only just begun."

She opened a notebook and drew a pie chart.

And Sky labeled it:

"The 50/30/20 Rule A Blueprint for Balance."

The Rule

50% Needs: Things you must pay for

Food, transportation, supplies.

30% Wants: Things you enjoy but can live without

Clothes, entertainment, fun.

20% Savings:

Money that is invested for emergencies, future opportunities.

Their Decision

They decided together to apply:

$2,500 (50%) — supplies, equipment, inventory as well as future events

$1,500 (30%) — celebration + food for volunteers

$1,000 (20%) — savings and emergency fund

“Budgeting isn’t about restriction,” Liam said.

“It’s about direction.”

And he was right that simple rule helped them keep on track

the next month, unexpected costs popped up.

But their savings kept the project alive.

ALLOWANCE
MON
TUE
WED
THU
FRI
SAT
SUN
SAVING
TO TAKE THE WORLD
YOU CAN'T SEE FAILURE AS PERMANENT ONLY AS A BUILDING BLOCK.
BUYSTORM
TEEN ALLOWANCE

Lesson for Readers

Budgeting gives you control.

Without a plan, your money controls you.

Activity

Write down your next allowance or paycheck.

Divide it using the 50/30/20 rule.

Then challenge yourself to follow it for 30 days.

Teen Affirmation

"Every dollar I get is a choice. I save to grow, I spend with purpose, and I give to make a difference."

Teen Allowance & Income Split Worksheet

Category	Recommended %	Purpose
Spending	50%	Things you want or need now
Saving / Investing	30%	For future goals, emergencies, growth
Sharing / Giving	20%	Helping others or supporting causes

Example with a $50 allowance

Spend: $25

Share: $15

Save: $10

Now complete your own:

Total Allowance or Income: $_____

Category	%	Amount	What I'll Do With It
Save			
Spend			
Share			

BILLS
50%
NEEDS
30%
WANTS
20%
SAVINGS
SAVING

Chapter 4: Allowances, Savings & Tracking Income

The thrift market had now turned into a weekly event.

Sky kept a small lockbox under the counter for earnings.

Liam recorded every sale in a notebook.

Andre made sure volunteers signed in.

Kimora labeled donation bins.

One day, Liam burst through the doors smiling.

"We made $1,800 this week."

Sky nodded. "Then let's split it right."

They divided their earnings like a paycheck:

50% — Operations fund (inventory, payroll)

30% — Group rewards (small stipends for volunteers)

20% — Group savings (their emergency stash)

“It’s not about dollars — it’s about discipline,” Andre said.

“We can’t build wealth if we don’t track it,” Sky added.

Kimora designed a colorful ledger with columns for:

Date

Description

Amount

Purpose

Every dollar was recorded.

They learned when sales went up when they dipped and what they could improve.

Lesson for Readers

Money grows where attention goes.

Try This

Start your own Money Journal.

Every time you earn or spend money, write it down.

At the end of the month, review it:

What helped me grow?

What slowed me down?

What will I change next month?

Teen Money Tracker & Bookkeeping Sheet

Step 1 Record Income & Expenses

Date	Description	Money In	Money Out

Step 2 Organize Your Spending

Category	**Total Spent ($)**	**Notes**
Needs		
Wants		
Savings / Investing		
Giving / Charity		

Step 3 Review Your Week

Did I save money this week?

Did I overspend?

What can I improve next week?

Teen Affirmation

"I don't guess where my money goes, I know. Every dollar has a job, and I'm the boss."

BILLS
PAYMENT SENT!
BILLS PAID

Chapter 5: Paying Debts & Earning Trust

It started with a simple deal.

Sky lent Andre $200 from the group fund to buy a new tool he needed.

“Pay me back after the weekend,” she said.

Story 1 The On-Time Payer

Andre sold old sneakers online and repaid Sky exactly when he said he would.

No reminders.

No excuses.

No stress.

The next time the group needed someone to handle money, they trusted Andre automatically.

Trust grows when you do what you say you will.

Story 2 The Late Payer

Liam borrowed $100 from Kimora one morning. He didn't forget he just kept saying:

"Tomorrow."

By the time he finally paid her back, Kimora wasn't angry just cautious.

So, when someone needed a loan later that month, she hesitated.

Late payments weaken confidence even when intentions are good.

Story 3 The Never Payer

Sky once lent $15 to a classmate for a school trip.

He never paid her back.

Months later, he asked to borrow money again.

Sky said no.

He lost more than $15 he lost trust.

Money lost can be earned back.

Trust lost can take years to rebuild.

Lesson for Readers

How you handle money shapes how people see your character.

Responsibility builds opportunities because reliable people get chosen first.

You don’t need to be perfect just consistent, honest, and dependable.

Activity

Think about the last time someone trusted you with money:

Did you return it on time?

Did you treat it like your own?

Did the other person feel confident in you afterward?

If not, start today!

Honor your word. Protect your name.

LEMONADE
50¢
TIPS

Chapter 6: Entrepreneurship & Creating Income Streams

When the community center repairs were nearly done, Sky had a new idea.

"What if we teach other kids how to earn too?"

They launched a Youth Market Day, booths for art, lemonade, cupcakes, and handmade jewelry.

Liam created flyers on his phone.

Kimora made eye-catching posters.

Andre built a wooden stand from scrap wood.

That weekend, they earned $3,500.

But more importantly…

They created jobs.

They created confidence.

They created ownership.

"When you make money from your ideas," Sky said,

"You stop waiting for someone to hand you a chance."

Entrepreneurship isn't about being rich.

It's about being resourceful.

It's turning what you have into something that serves others.

Lesson for Readers

Every young person has a product inside them:

A skill.

A service.

An idea people value.

Challenge

List three things you can do well.

Then ask yourself:

“How can I earn from one of these?”

Examples:

You draw? → Sell artwork or design T-shirts.

You bake? → Offer cupcakes for school events.

You’re good with tech? → Help neighbors set up phones or tablets.

Quote to Remember

"You don't need permission to build.

You need purpose."

— Gregory Smith

Chapter 7: The First Black Entrepreneur Clara Brown

Kimora was researching women leaders when she found a name she didn't recognize:

Clara Brown.

Born enslaved in Kentucky in the early 1800s, she earned her freedom and walked more than 600 miles to Colorado. She worked as a cook, a midwife, and a laundress, saving every coin until she eventually owned property and opened multiple successful businesses.

But Clara didn't stop there.

She used her money to help others, funding churches, supporting schools, and helping families reunite after slavery tore them apart.

"She didn't just build wealth," Sky said.

"She built legacy."

Inspired, the kids added Clara Brown to the mural wall inside the community center right beside Rosa Parks and Malcolm X.

Because wealth isn't just about money.

It's about using what you earn to lift your people.

Lesson for Readers

Black brilliance didn’t begin today.

Black entrepreneurship didn’t begin today.

We’ve always had the ability to build, create, and lead.

We just need the courage to act on it.

Activity

Research one historical figure who used business or leadership to create change.

Examples:

Madam C.J. Walker

Benjamin Banneker

Garrett Morgan

Maggie Lena Walker

Annie Malone

Alonzo Herndon

Write down:

What they did

What challenges they faced

How their story inspires your goals

Quote

“Be the proof that history continues through you.” — Gregory Smith

LEMONADE
CITY HALL
50¢
BUSINESS LICENSE
Chris Washington

Chapter 8: Taxes & Civil Responsibilities

The thrift market had grown into something bigger. Families from all over the neighborhood now came every weekend to shop, donate, and connect.

One afternoon, Mr. Howard, a city worker, stopped by their booth.

“You kids are doing great,” he said, smiling.

“But do you have a business license?”

Sky blinked. “A what?”

Mr. Howard chuckled gently. “When you start earning money, you must report it. That’s how we pay for schools, roads, parks, and yes even the community center you’re fixing up.”

Registering your business and obtaining your license allows you to pay taxes.

That conversation changed things.

Taxes weren’t this scary punishment adults complained about.

They were a form of participation.

Liam’s Research

Later that night, Liam looked it up:

Taxes help pay for:

Libraries

Teachers

Firefighters

Police and EMTs

Road repairs

School programs

Parks and recreation centers

After-school sports

"We all use the community," Andre said.

"So, we should all help support it."

Sky nodded.

"That's why learning this stuff matters. Money isn't just personal it's community."

Lesson for Readers

Paying taxes is a part of giving back.

It's how citizens help fund the systems that keep neighborhoods running.

You may not love taxes; nobody does, but you benefit from what they create every single day.

Activity

List five things in your city that exist because of taxes.

Then imagine a whole day without them.

Would your:

School,

Streets,

Wi-Fi at the library,

Playground,

Trash pickup,

Or school lunch program

still exist?

Probably not.

Understanding taxes helps you understand your responsibility as a citizen.

Quote

“Smart citizens don’t just earn they contribute.” Gregory Smith

VOTING

TAXES

Chapter 9: The Voting Rights Act of 1965 and Today

During social studies class, Kimora came across a line she couldn't ignore. She read it aloud to her brothers and sister later that afternoon:

"The Voting Rights Act of 1965 outlawed discriminatory practices that kept Black Americans from voting."

Liam frowned.

"Wait people were blocked from voting just because of their race?"

Sky nodded. "That's why our grandparents marched."

They visited the community library and found photographs of Dr. Martin Luther King Jr., John Lewis, and Fannie Lou Hamer. They saw crowds marching across the Edmund Pettus Bridge.

They read stories about people beaten, jailed, and even killed for trying to vote.

"Voting is wealth in another form," Andre said quietly.

"It's how we invest power."

Why Voting Still Matters Today

Even though the Voting Rights Act protected millions, new obstacles have appeared in modern times:

Strict ID laws

Closed polling places

Reduced early voting

Misinformation

Low voter turnout

Court decisions that weaken protections

The challenges may look different today, but the message is the same:

Your voice is your vote, and your vote shapes your future.

Lesson for Readers

Financial freedom means nothing without civic freedom.

Voting decides:

How schools are funded

Where community money goes

Who writes the laws

What resources your neighborhood gets

What opportunities your future will have

Your vote is a tool of protection and power.

Activity

Ask an adult in your family:

“Are you registered to vote?”

“When is the next election?”

“Why is voting important to you?”

Then research how you can register when you turn 18.

Promise yourself today:

I will never waste that right.

Quote

“Our ancestors paid for this right in blood; we honor them by showing up.” — Gregory Smith

THE VOTING RIGHTS ACT A 60-Year Journey

1965

The Voting Rights Act passes.

Ends literacy tests.

Protects Black voters.

Federal oversight begins in states with histories of discrimination.

2013 Shelby County v. Holder

The Supreme Court weakens the Act.

States with discrimination histories no longer need federal approval before changing voting laws.

2021 Brnovich v. DNC

Section 2 is limited.

It becomes harder to challenge discriminatory voting rules.

2025 New Challenges

The Supreme Court considers cases that could reduce protections even further.

Civil rights groups and citizens continue fighting to keep voting fair and equal.

Why It Matters

The right to vote didn't come easy.

People marched for it.

People bled for it.

People died for it.

That right remains one of the most powerful tools you will ever have.

Protect it.

Use it.

Understand its power.

MEDICAL CENTER

Chapter 10: Building Generational Wealth

Weeks later, the thrift market had its biggest day since Fab came through

$5,000 in sales.

Word had spread. Families showed up. Volunteers returned.

Two young entrepreneur book writers who have gained national exposure stopped by to show support.

But instead of celebrating, Sky called a team meeting.

“We can spend this,” she said,

"Or we can grow this."

Liam raised an eyebrow. "You're saying no snacks? No celebration?"

Andre laughed. "You know she's serious. Look at her face."

Sky smiled. "We'll celebrate. but smart. Because what we do with this money decides our future."

The First Investment

They decided to open a community savings account their very first investment.

Every week, they added:

Money from sales

Money from donations

The number grew slowly but steadily.

And with each deposit, the kids began to understand something deeper: Real wealth isn't about how much you make today, it's about what you build for tomorrow.

"It's Not About One Check…"

One afternoon, Liam stared at the growing balance.

"You know what?" he said.

"It's not about one check.

It's about what we leave behind."

Sky nodded.

"That's generational wealth."

Generational wealth means creating

Property

Savings

Businesses

Knowledge

Habits

Values

It means your children start where you finished not where you started.

Lesson for Readers

Money fades when it is only spent.

Legacy lasts when it is:

managed

protected

shared

taught

Generational wealth is a mindset passed from one generation to the next.

Steps to Start Generational Wealth

Save consistently even small amounts grow over time.

Learn before you spend; knowledge is the foundation of wealth.

Buy or build things that grow in value education, property, business, investments.

Teach what you learn; wealth grows when more hands know how to hold it.

Quote

"Generational wealth is a mindset passed from one generation to the next. " Gregory Smith

Chapter 11: Family, Manhood & Womanhood

The community center was finally alive again.

Fresh paint covered the walls.

The new mural of Clara Brown stood proudly beside portraits representing Sky, Liam, Andre, and Kimora.

Children played. Parents smiled. Music echoed across the hall.

Sky looked around and whispered, "We did it."

Andre nodded. "We built it."

That night, before locking up, the group sat together in a circle inside the now-transformed space.

They had learned about money, yes.

But they had learned far more about themselves.

Sky

"Being a young woman doesn't mean waiting for someone to lead. It means leading with love, wisdom, and confidence. We set examples for our sisters, our brothers, and our community."

Liam

"Being a young man isn't about being the loudest or the toughest. It's about being steady. Taking responsibility. Protecting what's right. Keeping your word."

Andre

"Family isn't only blood. Family is who shows up, who believes in you, and who works beside you. That's what makes us strong."

Kimora

"Womanhood isn't weakness it's grace under pressure.

Manhood isn't about control its about respect."

They realized something important:

Wealth without values is empty.

Money can buy comfort.

Character builds community.

And when young men and young women learn to honor one another, families grow and so does the world around them.

Lesson for Readers

Your first business is your family.

Your first partnership is built on trust.

Your character not your money will always determine how far your name goes.

Reflection Activity

Write one promise to your family that will make them proud in ten years.

Then write one promise to yourself and keep it!

Quote

"When men lead with wisdom and women lead with love, wealth becomes generational."

Gregory Smith

Walking in Purpose: Knowing Who You Are and Who You're Becoming

For Every Young Girl Learning to Walk in Her Power and Her Faith

Walking in purpose means learning who you are not just who people say you should be. It's understanding that your life has meaning, and your voice has weight. You are not here by accident. Whether you see it through faith or through the story of where you come from, your existence carries power.

From the beginning, women have been made with purpose to create, to nurture, to build, and to lead with love. And as a girl, you carry that purpose with an extra layer of strength. It's in your voice when you speak up. It's in your walk when you step into a room that wasn't built for you, but you still make space for yourself. It's in your roots the laughter, lessons, and legacy of women before you who prayed, worked, dreamed, and made a way.

Walking in purpose doesn't always feel easy. Sometimes you'll question if you're enough if you fit in, if you're ready, if you belong. But walking in purpose means choosing to trust that you already have everything you need inside of you. It's knowing that God, the universe, or simply your inner strength is guiding you even when you can't see the whole picture.

Purpose isn't just in the big moments. It's in the everyday choices how you treat people, how you speak to yourself, how you decide to keep showing up. It's in the way you protect your peace, forgive when it's hard, and believe that your dreams are valid no matter what anyone says.

Walking in purpose means being present, not perfect. It's learning from your mistakes, standing tall after you fall, and letting your light shine even when the world feels dark. It's saying, "I'm still here, and I'm still becoming."

As a young woman, you are part of a story that stretches back generations one of beauty, brilliance, and resilience. You carry both your ancestors' prayers and your own possibilities. You are both grounded and growing.

When you walk in purpose, you walk in peace. You start to understand that womanhood isn't about competition or perfection it's about connection, compassion, and courage. You are meant to take up space, to lead with love, and to live boldly.

Because your purpose isn't waiting on you to be someone else it's waiting on you to be you.

Chapter 11.5: Liam Reads the Words of Manhood

As the evening grew quiet inside the community center, the team cleaned up the last of their tools.

On a bulletin board half hidden behind a layer of dust Liam spotted a framed page titled “Manhood.”

He pulled it down gently, and the group gathered as he began to read.

Manhood

A man positions himself so that observation comes before reaction, where study is preferred to nightlife, and emotion is not seen as weakness.

Love for self is love for family and children making your life accessible to them in meaningful ways.

A man is willing to share resources fully.

He struggles unrelentingly against the evils of the world, especially those that threaten the growth of his people.

A man seeks to be what is just, good, and correct.

He is a listener, a student, a seeker of truth, and he demands the same from those who lead him.

He protects the weak.

He respects his elders.

He stays spiritually connected to what is good and right. A man is a committed partner sensitive to his woman's needs and aspirations, knowing nothing should interrupt the communication between them.

A man loves life and all that is beautiful.

He grows constantly and learns from mistakes. He is soft and strong, never afraid to take the lead.

When Liam finished reading, the room stayed still.

Sky nodded. “That’s not just about men,” she said softly. “That’s about being a real human being.”

Andre looked thoughtful. “I’m gonna try to live up to that.”

They placed the frame back on the wall not as decoration, but as direction.

Quote

“Manhood isn’t about being perfect it’s about being present, accountable, and awake.”

Greg Smith

The Importance of History, Family, and the Unity of Siblings

1. Understanding Family History

Family history is the story of where you come from the people, traditions, and experiences that shaped your identity.

Knowing your history gives you:

Identity

It helps you understand who you are and where your strength comes from.

Gratitude

Every generation before you sacrificed, struggled, or worked so you could have more than they did.

Wisdom

Lessons from elders can help you avoid mistakes and make better decisions.

Activity

Interview an older family member.

Write down three things you learned about your family's past.

2. The Role of Family

Family is the first team you ever join.

It's the people who guide you, support you, challenge you, and love you unconditionally.

Why family matters:

Family teaches values like respect, empathy, and responsibility.

Family becomes your support system when life gets difficult.

Strong families help create stronger individuals and stronger communities.

Discussion

What is one value your family has taught you that you want to carry into adulthood?

3. The Unity of Siblings

Siblings share more than a home they share roots.

They're your first lifelong teammates.

Why sibling unity matters:

Protection: You look out for one another.

Support: You celebrate each other's wins and help each other grow.

Legacy: The way you treat each other teaches future generations what family should look like.

Think of siblings like fingers on a hand one finger alone is weak, but together, they can do powerful things.

Activity

Work together on one small goal:

Cook a meal

Clean a room

Write a family poem

Help a parent

Organize a space

Then talk about how teamwork helped.

FREEDOM
MINDS
OPEN
DAY
STORM
TO TAKE THE WORLD
YOU CAN'T SEE
BLOCK.

A Young Man's Role with His Siblings and His Family

1. What It Means to Be a Young Man

Being a young man isn't about being the strongest or the loudest.

It's about how you:

Lead

Protect

Respect

And Grow

Your family needs young men who are dependable, thoughtful, and kind.

Your role includes:

Being an example; showing your siblings how to do the right thing even when no one is watching.

Being a helper; stepping in when your family needs support whether that's chores encouragement or just showing up.

Being a learner; listening to elders and growing in wisdom.

2. Your Role with Your Sisters

Your sisters older or younger often look to you for cues on how men should treat them.

What you owe them:

Respect: treat them with dignity your actions teach them what kind of respect to expect from other men.

Protection: stand up for them if someone disrespects them.

Support: celebrate their wins and be someone they can trust. Example: If your sister has a big test ask if she needs help or encouragement, small things build trust.

3. Your Role with Your Brothers

Your brothers are teammates for life. You don't have to be the same, but you can always have each other's back.

Be the kind of brother who:

Pushes them to do better

Corrects them privately but praises them publicly

Works with them, not against them

no jealousy, no competition

Iron sharpens iron.

Strong brothers make strong men.

4. Your Role in the Whole Family

Every family needs people who bring peace and unity.

A young man shows leadership through:

Dependability: doing what you said you'd do

Respect: using kind words, even when angry

Presence: putting the phone down and being there

Gratitude: thanking the people who care for you

5. Final Thought

"Being a man starts at home in how you treat your family, protect your sisters, support your brothers, and honor your parents."

You don't need to be perfect.

You just have to show up, care, and grow.

STORM

A Young Lady's Role with Her Siblings and Her Family

1. What It Means to Be a Young Lady

Being a young lady is more than growing older.

It means learning to carry yourself with:

Grace

Strength

Purpose

And love

You are an essential part of the foundation of your family.

Your role includes:

Kindness: showing compassion even when it's difficult.

Responsibility: taking ownership of your choices.

Confidence: knowing your worth and encouraging others to see theirs.

2. Your Role with Your Siblings

Your brothers and sisters look up to you in ways you may not realize. The way you treat them helps shape how they treat others.

What you owe them:

Patience: younger siblings are still learning.

Encouragement: celebrates their wins, big or small.

Unity: helps bring peace to the home, not conflict.

3. Your Role with Your Brothers

Your brothers learn how to treat women by how you carry yourself.

What you can do:

Show self-respect so they know how to value women and themselves.

Encourage them remind them of their strengths.

Work together be teammates, not rivals.

4. Your Role in the Whole Family

Young ladies bring:

Warmth

Creativity

Compassion

Clarity

Strength

Your presence helps shape the home.

You can:

Be respectful to parents and elders

Be dependable, do your part without being asked

Be supportive, lift your family when they're down

Be proud, represent your family well

5. Final Thought

"A young lady's strength is shown through her kindness, her confidence, and her love for her family."

Being graceful and strong starts at home.

Chapter 12: The Final Reflection: The Real Return

The night was quiet when Sky, Liam, Andre, and Kimora locked up the community center. Fresh paint still carried its scent, and pride lingered in every corner. The same cracked sidewalks they walked across months earlier now looked different like possibilities waiting to be paved.

It wasn't just about repairs.

It never really was.

They didn't just raise money.

They raised standards.

They didn't just paint the walls.

They painted a new mindset one where young people saw themselves as the answer instead of waiting for one.

They didn't just sell thrift items.

They sold hope, piece by piece, until the community started to believe again.

Sky looked back at the mural a swirl of color, faces, and history.

“You know what?” she whispered.

“This place isn’t just fixed. It’s alive.”

Liam nodded, hands in his pockets.

“Feels different when you build something instead of just using it.”

Andre grinned.

“Yeah… because when you build something, you understand what it’s worth.”

Kimora smiled.

“And you protect it.”

They stood there in silence, letting the moment settle.

What They Learned

They learned that every dollar carries a decision and that smart money starts with self-respect.

They learned that unity pays interest because teamwork builds more than bank accounts.

They learned that wealth without wisdom is just noise and that discipline turns dreams into direction.

They learned that it's not about how much you make but what you make of what you have.

Most of all, they learned that what you do with your money says a lot, but what you do with your heart says everything.

The Real Investment

Sky spoke first.

"This whole project started with a broken building… but maybe that was the point.

We had to rebuild ourselves first."

Liam smiled.

"It's crazy. We spent all this time learning about money, but what we really learned was character."

Andre nodded.

"Yeah… responsibility. Trust. Teamwork.

That's the real currency."

Kimora added,

"And giving back.

That's the kind of wealth that never runs out."

They locked the doors and started walking home.

The moonlight traced their shadows across the street long, connected, stretching ahead like generations reaching forward.

Sky turned around one last time.

"We did good," she whispered.

Liam placed a hand on her shoulder.

"Nah," he said.

"We started something."

Andre laughed.

"Yeah. We're not done we're just cashing in the first return."

Kimora grinned.

"And it's worth more than money."

The Lesson

The world teaches you how to earn but not always how to value.

Their journey in this book was never just about chasing cash.

It was about chasing clarity.

Dollars & Sense isn't just about the math of money.

It's about the mindset behind it.

Because every dollar you touch reflects how much you respect:

yourself

your time

your purpose

And every wise choice adds interest to your legacy.

Legacy Note

When the lights went out at the community center, something brighter turned on inside them, a light that can't be unplugged.

They finally understood what Pops meant:

"Money doesn't make the man the man makes the money."

And in that moment, they became the proof.

They built wealth the way it was meant to be built through wisdom, work, and love.

Their story became the story of Dollars & Sense itself: a reminder that when you use your gifts to lift others, the profit is permanent.

Epilogue: The Legacy We Build

Liam speaking:

"I can't believe this just dropped into our hands," Liam said, eyes wide with disbelief and excitement. "It's like everything Pops has been telling us for years is finally connecting."

He smirked and stretched. "I think I'm gonna hit the gym. That treadmill time! That's when my mind really opens up. Ideas just start flowing."

There was something powerful about that moment the realization that this journey wasn't just about money.

It was about everything.

Pops' lessons weren't just stories; they were blueprints. And now, those blueprints were finally making sense.

Kimora leaned forward, voice steady and thoughtful.

"There are parts of life people don't talk about the raw stuff," she said. "Like growing up with the prison experience."

She paused, letting the truth settle.

"I'm not saying every family needs to go through it. But maybe… if more people understood what it's really like not the TV version they'd think twice about the choices they make. Because what's a 'slap on the wrist' for some, could be a juvenile sentence for us."

She inhaled slowly.

"We've lived it. Felt it. And the system sees us differently before we even open our mouths. That's why this book matters. If we're going to tell the truth, we can't leave out the parts that shaped us even the painful ones."

Sky looked out the window, eyes softening.

"Shout out to Uncle Andre. One of the smartest, most talented people I know. I wish he was home."

Andre's voice dropped low.

"I think about Uncle Dre all the time. I'm named after him. He really is one of the most gifted people I've ever

known…"

He swallowed.

"But he's not here. He's not home."

Liam placed a hand on his shoulder.

"You carry his name, bro. And you carry his light. That's real."

Sky sat forward.

"And while we're telling the truth we need to talk about health and wellness. Every human need that lesson."

Kimora nodded.

"Facts. We don't talk about it enough, especially in our community."

Sky continued:

"We normalize stress. We normalize pain. We eat whatever, sleep whenever, and ignore warning signs. But health isn't optional it's foundational."

Andre added,

"Kids my age are already dealing with anxiety, depression, even high blood pressure."

Liam rubbed the back of his neck.

"People think working out is just about looking good. Nah. It's about clarity. When I run, my thoughts get straight."

Sky nodded.

“It’s all connected. You can’t chase dreams with a tired mind and a weak body. You can’t lead if you’re running on empty. You can’t show up for others if you’re not showing up for yourself.”

She laughed lightly, then turned serious again.

“So yeah this book needs to talk about wellness. That’s not optional. That’s the base.”

Andre shifted forward.

“We’ve all had different paths different mothers, different homes. But we share a name, a legacy, and a responsibility.”

He swallowed.

“Uncle Dre used to say, ‘Family isn’t just who you’re born to it’s who you show up for.’ And I’ve been thinking about that a lot. We gotta show up… for the ones who didn’t get the chance, and the ones still coming.”

He looked at the group.

“But let’s not forget none of this happens without Him. The Highest Power. He’s the one who aligned our steps. Who gave us the chance to be more than statistics.”

Andre finished softly:

"The Smith legacy is rooted in family, community, and unity guided by faith. That's what Dollars & Sense is about.

Not just money.

Not just hustle.

But meaning."

Sky nodded:

"We're building something that outlives us. Something real."

And in that quiet moment, they understood:

Their story wasn't just theirs.

It was a legacy in motion.

Final Words from Greg Smith

"You are the next generation of thinkers, creators, and leaders.

What you do with your mind will determine what you do with your money.

Make both count."

Greg Smith

"Wealth begins in the mind, grows through discipline, and lasts through love."

Greg Smith

Teen Affirmations

"I build assets, not debt. My money works for me not the other way around."

"Every dollar I get is a choice. I save to grow, I spend with purpose, and I give to make a difference."

"I don't guess where my money goes I know. Every dollar has a job, and I'm the boss."

"My ideas have value. My effort creates opportunity."

"I can't control where I start, but I can control how I finish."

"My mind is my first investment. Learning is my wealth."

"I am building something that will outlive me."

"I show up for myself, my family, and my future."

"Money isn't my identity it's my tool for impact."

Glossary of Key Terms

Asset — Something that puts money in your pocket or grows in value.

Liability — Something that costs you money or loses value.

Budget — A plan for how you spend, save, and give money intentionally.

50/30/20 Rule — 50% needs, 30% wants, 20% savings.

Allowance — Regular money received to practice managing finances.

Entrepreneur — A person who uses ideas or skills to earn money and serve others.

Generational Wealth — Money, property, or knowledge passed down.

Investment — Using money today to grow more tomorrow.

Interest — Extra money earned or owed when money is saved or borrowed.

Credit — Borrowed money that must be repaid with interest; builds financial trust.

Legacy — What you leave behind that helps others money, wisdom, or impact.

Resources & Activities

1. Financial Practice

Track allowance

List assets vs. liabilities

Start a money journal

2. Entrepreneurship

Create a mini business stand

Track earnings

Reflect on your business decisions

3. Civic & Community Learning

Volunteer locally

Learn how taxes and voting shape your community

4. Personal Growth

Build a daily wellness routine

Practice emotional, mental, and physical self-care

5. Community Resources

MyMoney.gov

Junior Achievement

FDIC Money Smart

Buystorm LLC

Final Reflection

"You have everything you need to build wealth your mind, your effort, and your heart.

Use them wisely.

Lead with purpose.

Leave something behind that matters."

www.ingramcontent.com/pod-product-compliance
Lightning Source LLC
LaVergne TN
LVHW010836120826
845149LV00017B/1473

* 9 7 9 8 9 9 4 4 5 2 2 0 2 *